SHARKS

SHARKS

Sarah Creese

make
believe
ideas

Sleek sharks are short and long,
large and fast and fierce and strong.
Beware the pointed, big shark fin,
a powerful tail, and a toothy grin!

Reading together

This book is an ideal first reader for your child, combining simple words and sentences with stunning color photography of real-life sharks. Here are some of the many ways you can help your child take those first steps in reading. Encourage your child to:

- Look at and explore the detail in the pictures.

- Sound out the letters in each word.

- Read and repeat each short sentence.

Look at the pictures

Make the most of each page by talking about the pictures and finding key words. Here are some questions you can use to discuss each page as you go along:

- Why do you like this shark?

- What is special about it?

- Where does it live?

- What does it eat?

Look at rhymes

Some of the sentences in this book are simple rhymes. Encourage your child to recognize rhyming words. Try asking the following questions:

- What does this word say?

- Can you find a word that rhymes with it?

- Look at the ending of two words that rhyme. Are they spelled the same? For example, "meal" and "seal," and "teeth" and "reef."

Test understanding

It is one thing to understand the meaning of individual words, but you need to make sure that your child understands the facts in the text.

- Play "find the obvious mistake." Read the text as your child looks at the words with you, but make an obvious mistake to see if he or she catches it. Ask your child to correct you and provide the right word.

- After reading the facts, close the book and think up questions to ask your child.

- Make statements about the sharks and ask your child whether the statements are true or false.

- Provide your child with three answers to a question and ask him or her to pick the correct one.

Quiz pages

At the end of the book there is a simple quiz. Ask the questions and see if your child can remember the right answers from the text. If not, encourage him or her to look up the answers.

Sharks

Amazing sharks live in oceans around the world.

With a mouth full of sharp teeth, sharks are deadly hunters of the sea.

I'm a great white shark.
I'm white and gray.
A strong sense of smell
helps me hunt my prey.

Splash!

With sharp, pointed teeth,
I catch a meal—
some fish, a sea lion,
a whale or a seal!

Did you know?

Sharks have many rows of teeth in their mouth. When a tooth gets damaged, another tooth is ready to replace it.

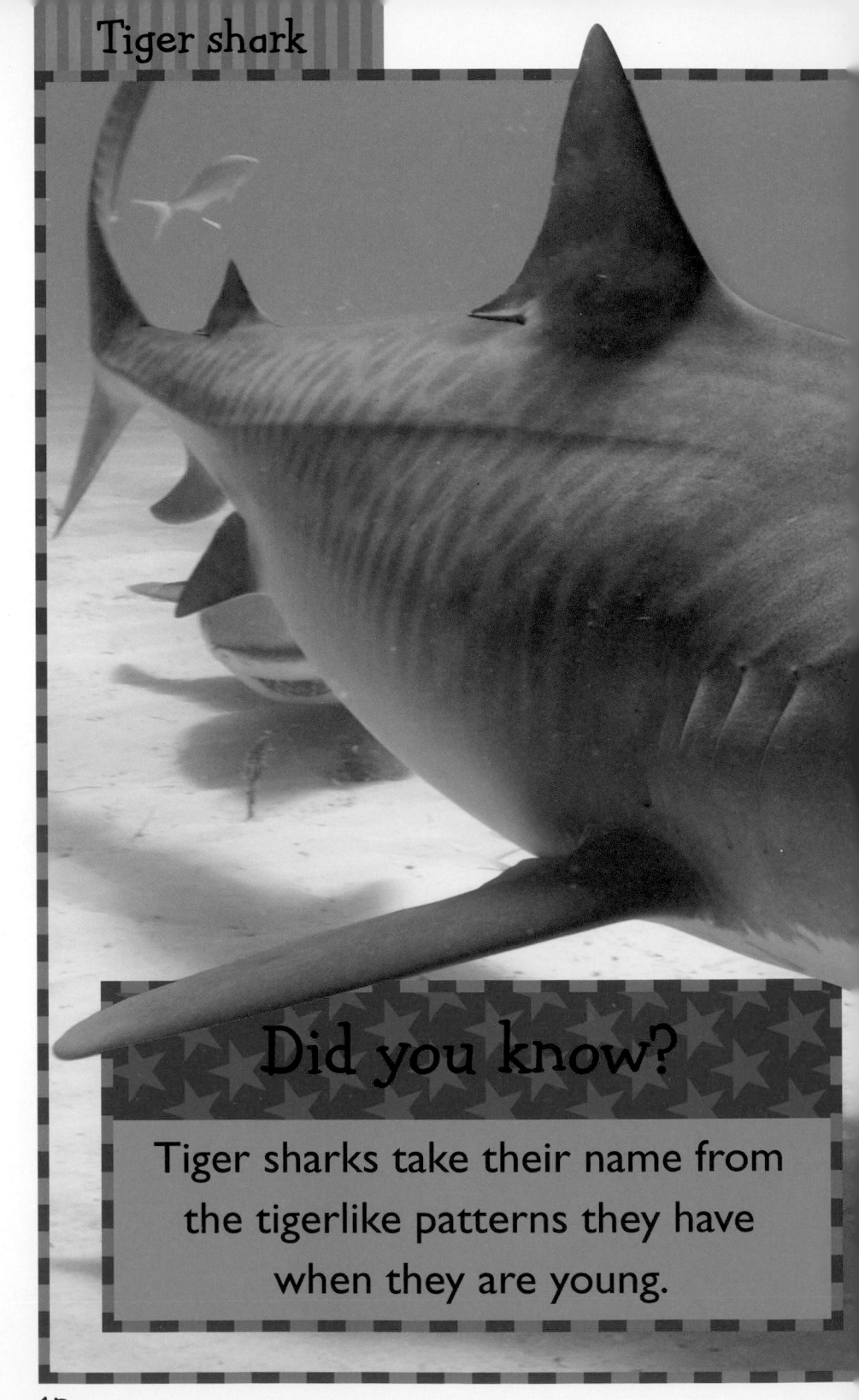

Did you know?

Tiger sharks take their name from the tigerlike patterns they have when they are young.

I'm a tiger shark,
I like to hunt alone.
My tiger stripes will fade
when I'm fully grown.

I'm a shark
with a rectangular head.
I attack stingrays
on the seabed!

Did you know?

Hammerheads' eyes are wide apart. This helps them to see more than other sharks.

I'm the world's largest fish,
but I'm as harmless as can be.
I'm a massive whale shark.
There's none bigger than me.

I rest in the day
with other nurse sharks.
When nighttime comes,
I hunt in the dark!

Did you know?

Nurse sharks live in warm,
shallow water. They swim slowly
at the bottom of the sea.

With long, thin teeth,
I eat my favorite dish,
a tasty meal of
wriggly reef fish.

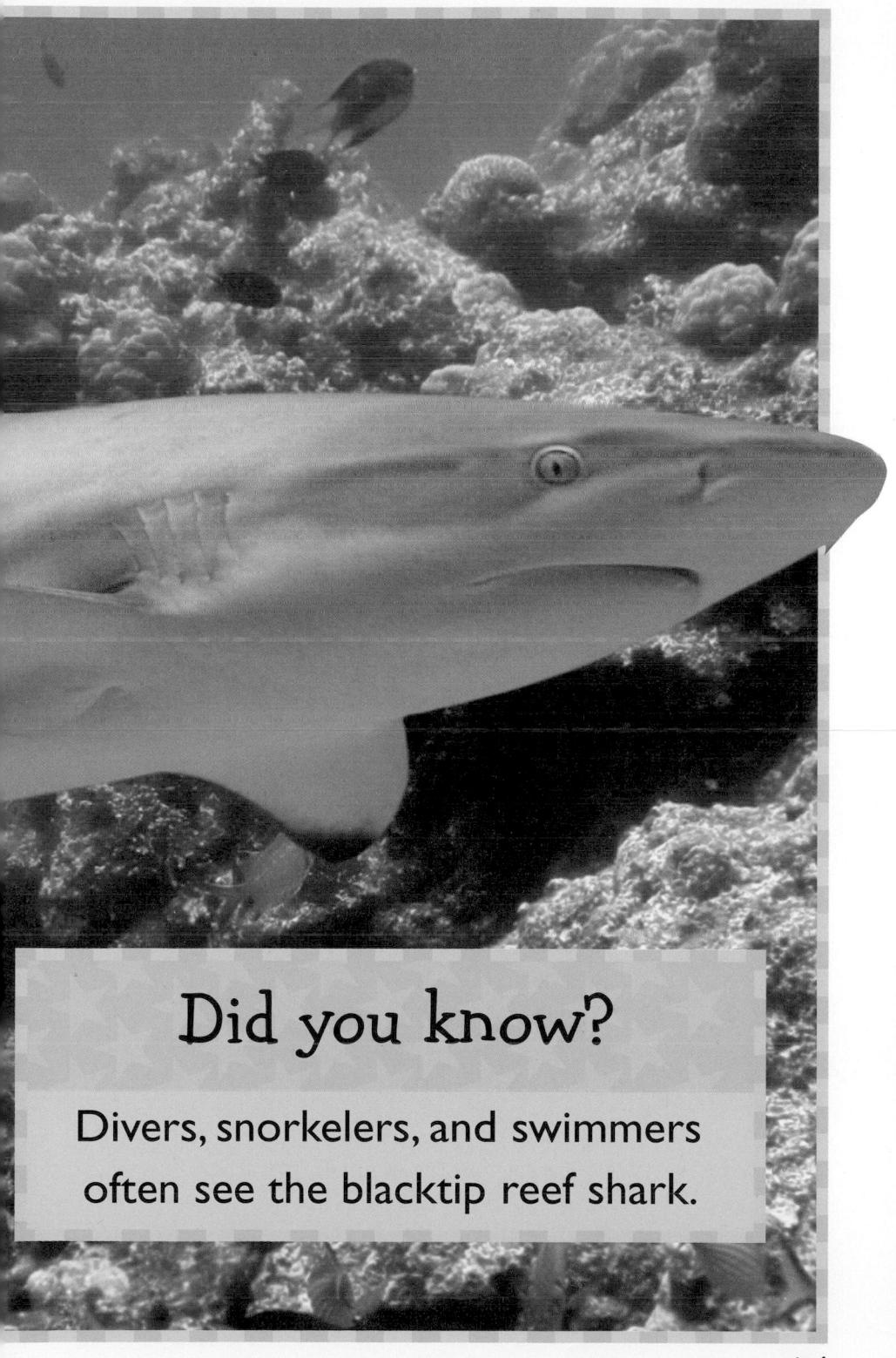

Did you know?

Divers, snorkelers, and swimmers often see the blacktip reef shark.

I swim smoothly
around the coral reef.
Look out for my black fins
and super sharp teeth.

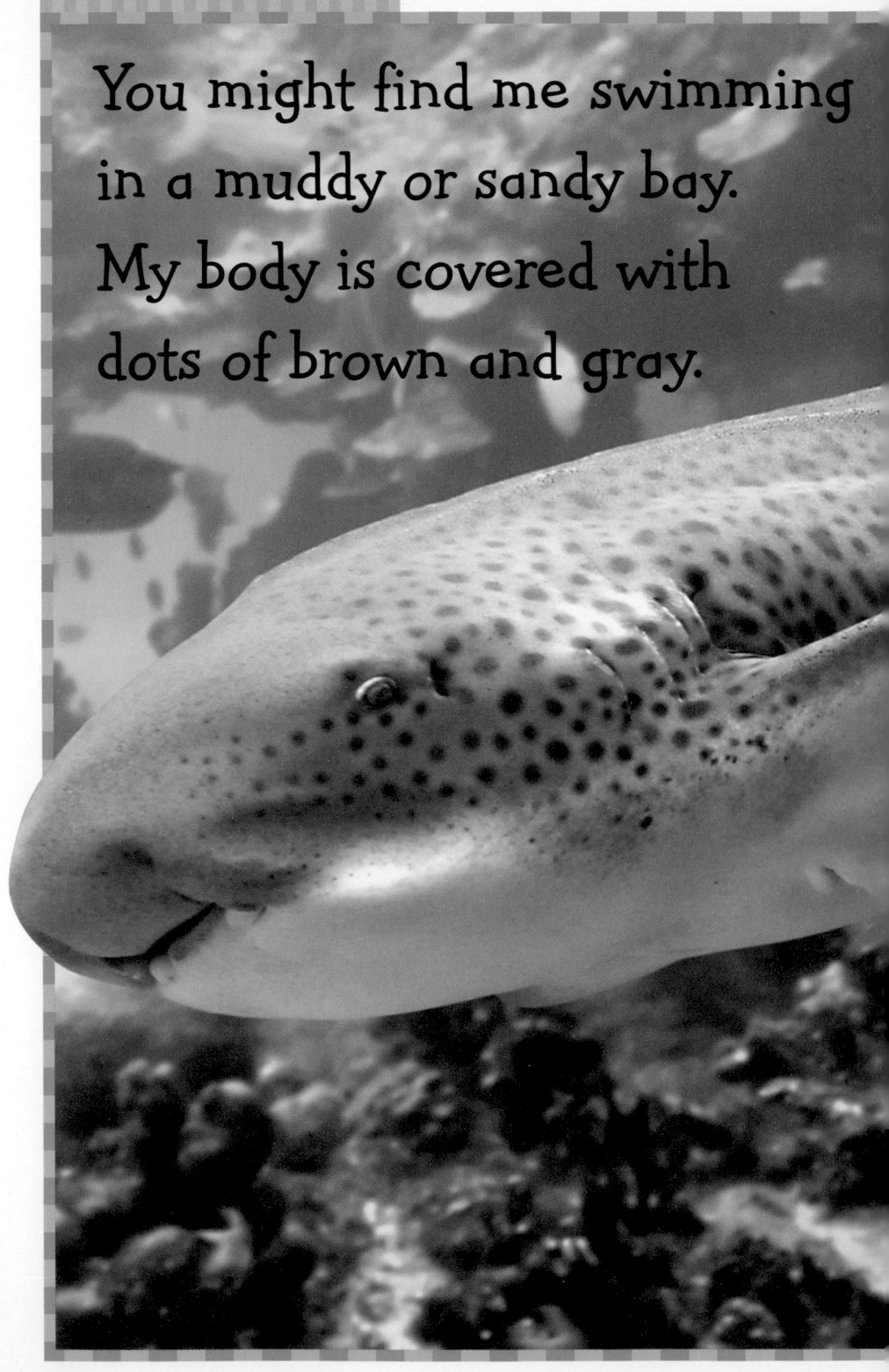

You might find me swimming in a muddy or sandy bay. My body is covered with dots of brown and gray.

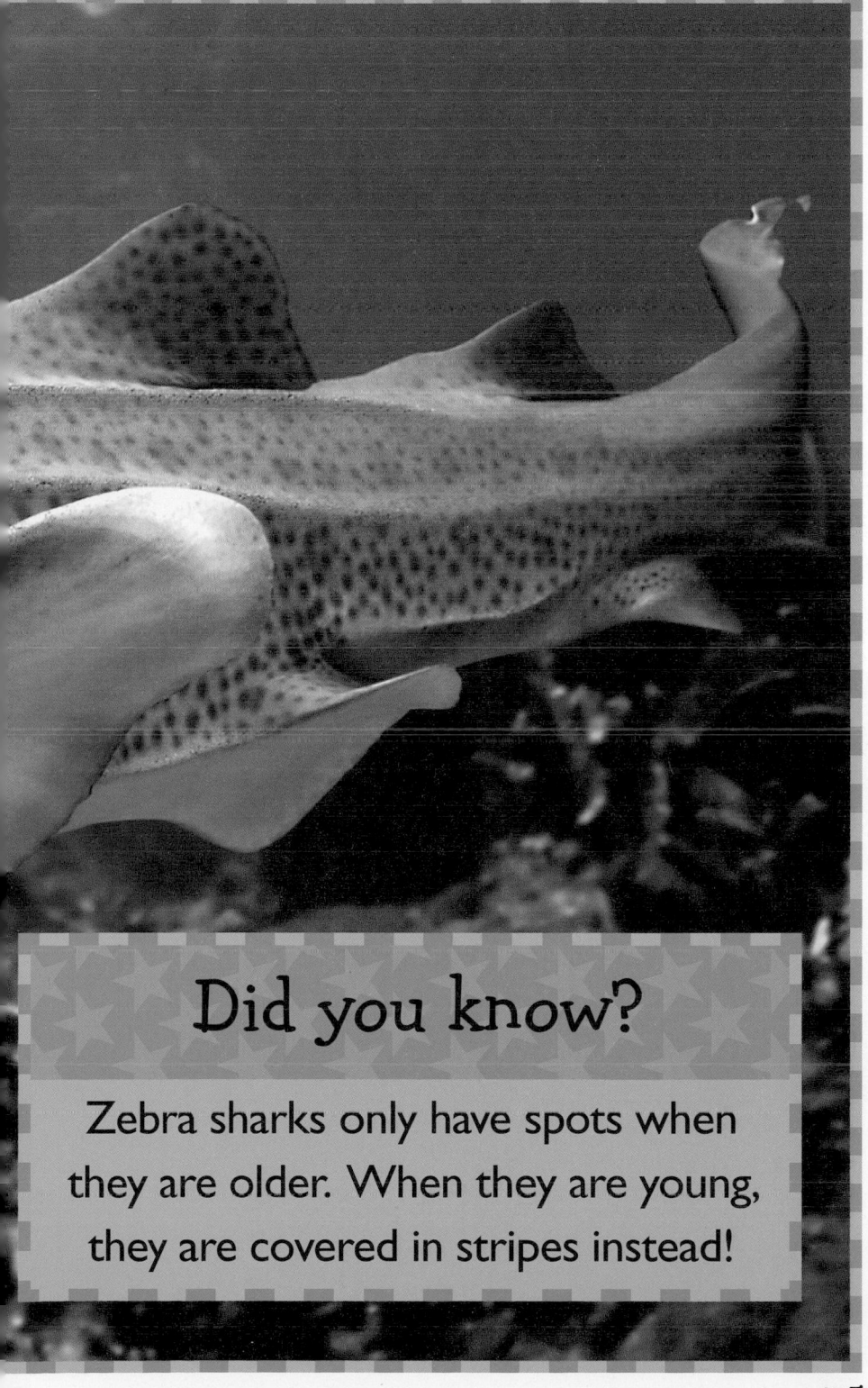

Did you know?

Zebra sharks only have spots when they are older. When they are young, they are covered in stripes instead!

I'm a powerful bull shark.
My snout is short and blunt.
Shallow water and rivers
are where I like to hunt!

Did you know?

The bull shark has been known to bump other sharks and divers if it thinks they are both trying to catch the same prey!

What do you know?

1. Which shark is the largest fish in the world?

2. Which shark's snout is short and blunt?

3. When does a nurse shark hunt?

4. What pattern does a young zebra shark have on its body?

5. What shape is a hammerhead shark's head?

6. In what type of water does a nurse shark live?

7. What color is a great white shark?

8. Which shark can hunt in rivers?

9. What pattern does an adult zebra shark have on its body?

10. Which shark has eyes that are wide apart?

11. What do great white sharks like to eat?

12. Which shark likes to swim around the coral reef?

Dictionary

fin

Fish have fins to help them swim, steer, and balance.

stingray

A stingray is a flat fish with a long tail. It can be found at the bottom of the seabed.

hunt

To hunt another animal is to chase and eat it.

pointed

Things that are pointed get thinner towards their tip. They can also be sharp.

blunt

If something is blunt it does not have a sharp point.

Key words

Here are some key words used in context.
Make simple sentences for the other
words in the border.

I **like** to eat stingrays.

I swim smoothly.

My teeth are sharp.

I **have** a striped body.

I am **the**
largest fish.